Music Instruction

The Nashville Numbering System

An Aid to Playing by Ear

by Neal Matthews Jr.

I'd like to extend a special thank you to Donna Hilley, who is the current president and CEO of Sony/ATV Music Publishing in Nashville. Donna encouraged me to write this book and introduced me to the Hal Leonard Corporation, who saw the merits of my publication and decided to put it into print. Donna is a true friend and I am eternally grateful to her.

—Neal Matthews Jr.

ISBN 978-0-88188-335-5

HAL•LEONARD®
CORPORATION
7777 W. BLUEMOUND RD. P.O. BOX 13819 MILWAUKEE, WI 53213

Visit Hal Leonard Online at
www.halleonard.com

Preface

The Nashville numbering system, often called the "Nashville shorthand" by outside artists recording in Music City, played an important role in the growth and development of the "Nashville sound." It is an abbreviated form of a normal arrangement of a song, giving each note in the scale a number, the way "Do-Re-Mi" gives each note a sound, enabling one to quickly learn a song in its entirety by ear.

Music is probably the most popular art form of our time, simply because so many are able to participate in it in one way or another. It seems that almost everyone possesses some innate musical knowledge or ability, whether it be to perform for others' enjoyment or simply to listen and enjoy good music with a certain degree of intelligence.

It has been said that inside every person there lies a hit song just waiting to be born. Story after story has emerged from Music Row in Nashville about people who walked into recording and publishing companies from off the street and immediately became superstars or successful songwriters. True, this has happened more than once in Music City, but the odds are definitely stacked against this sort of thing, for music is a highly competitive field. But, if a person possesses certain musical abilities, such as an ability to recognize differences in sound, especially in rhythm, pitch, or musical tones, this person would "have a good ear" for music. Such a person could definitely be trained to sing or play a musical instrument by ear.

There are numerous people who have some limited natural ability in music, but who have never had the opportunity to develop or improve their talents through voice lessons or through the many available instruments, such as piano or guitar. These are essentially the type of people I am trying to reach in the following pages. Learning music by ear with the aid of the Nashville numbering system should be simple and lots of fun, not complicated and mind-boggling. This is not to say that no work is involved. As we all know, anything worthwhile requires work and practice in order for a person to be proficient, but the reward of reaching your own chosen degree of success is well worth the effort.

I emphasize the guitar in this book, for it is guitarists, especially, who have found the Nashville numbering system to be useful. Those of you who already play the guitar can greatly enhance your ability to learn new songs quickly as you develop the "Nashville shorthand" taught in this book. Those of you who have musical ability but have never played the guitar can actually get started playing by taking some of the basic steps described in the following pages.

Therefore, if that hit song is lurking somewhere deep within, and you simply have not acquired the formal training or developed the natural ability necessary to dig it out by using your ear, I intend to explore some ways to help you better understand the "sights and sounds" of music; and, in doing so, I hope to make your quest for greatness a trifle easier.

I do not promise you a hit song, and I do not promise to make you a superstar, but I do promise that a thorough trip through these pages will not only be interesting but informative as well.

My purpose is to help you to better understand music in general and the guitar in particular by using your own natural abilities to the fullest. I believe that the Nashville numbering system can do this; and, should this goal be reached, then the purpose for having written this book will have been achieved.

CONTENTS

Background:
Neal Matthews Jr. and the Jordanaires

Born in Nashville, Neal Matthews Jr. has played guitar and sung as long as he can remember. His dad played guitar and "taught us western and gospel songs from the time we were cutting our first teeth." By age ten, Neal, his brother Roger, and his cousin Rachel were singing at banquets and theaters. By age thirteen, he was playing with his dad in a band on the Grand Ole Opry.

After graduating from Hume Fogg High School in Nashville, he sang and played guitar with "Wally Fowler and the Oak Ridge Quartet," which eventually evolved into the present "Oak Ridge Boys," although the personnel has changed several times down through the years.

Beginning in 1951, he served a twenty-one-month hitch in the army. He was decorated in Korea with a bronze star. Shortly after returnng home (1953), he joined the Jordanaires and mixed singing with two years of school at Belmont College in Nashville. His college career was cut short in 1956 when Elvis Presley wanted the Jordanaires to accompany all his road appearances, plus his recording and movie sound tracks.

Neal Matthews Jr.

Neal still plays guitar on occasion when the group performs in public. He also does the session arranging for the group, and it was in this capacity that he developed the Nashville numbering system.

He lives in the Brentwood community, which lies just south of Nashville, with his family —wife Charlsie, daughter Lisa, and son Greg. To them he gives much of the credit for this first endeavor in writing a book, attesting that they have contributed "in both moral and manual support."

The Jordanaires quartet is one of the busiest and most versatile vocal groups in the music world today. They are familiar to almost everyone who listens to the radio, plays records, watches television, or goes to the movies, because they have been involved in all aspects of the communications industry for more than twenty-five years. Composed of four men whose voices are heard on thirty to fifty million records each year, the Jordanaires perform all across the musical spectrum — country and western, popular and semi-popular, barbershop and spirituals, rock and roll, and radio and television commercials — whatever the producer requires. It was religious music, especially spirituals, that gave the Jordanaires their name. In 1957 they gained national recognition by winning on Arthur Godfrey's "Talent Scouts" show with one of their spirituals. Their close harmony later became an integral part of the many hit records of Elvis Presley, who "dug" their spirituals so much that he asked them to work with him, bringing the quartet international attention.

All members of the group play instruments, and in those early years they provided both vocal and instrumental music on Elvis' records. For fourteen years, the Jordanaires provided backing on all of Presley's records. The sales ranked in the millions, and in the process they established their own careers, until today this quartet is perhaps the most-heard vocal backing group in the nation. On television they have appeared with Tennessee Ernie Ford, Milton Berle, Ed Sullivan (their first network appearance), Eddy Arnold, and many other outstanding entertainers. The group made twenty-eight movies with Elvis, and were regularly featured on the Grand Ole Opry for thirteen years. They have been repeatedly listed by the international music trade publications as one of the most popular singing groups in the world. They provide vocal background on many hit albums and singles with such stars as Marty Robbins, Ronnie Milsap, Kenny Rogers, Jim Reeves, Ringo Starr, Johnny Cash, Lynn Anderson, Loretta Lynn, Charley Pride, Steve Lawrence and Eydie Gorme, B.J. Thomas, Tennessee Ernie Ford, Crystal Gayle, Barbara Mandrell, and, of course, Elvis Presley.

Each member of the group resides with his family in or around Nashville, Tennessee. The Jordanaires, as we know them — Gordon Stoker (leader), Neal Matthews, and Hoyt Hawkins — began vocal background singing in the early 1950s, and in 1958 the group was completed with the addition of Ray Walker. With a history of such versatile success, it is no wonder that these four outstanding performers have been together longer than any vocal group active today.

The Jordanaires won the 1979 National Academy of Recording Arts and Sciences Award ("Grammy") for having sung on more top ten recordings than any other group. The number one record in this award was Kenny Rogers' "The Gambler." The Jordanaires also contributed to the winning entries in the 1980 Academy of Country Music Awards for Single Record of Year — George Jones' "He Stopped Loving Her Today" — and Top Vocal Duet — Moe Bandy and Joe Stampley.

Birth of the Numbering System in Nashville

In the mid-fifties the Jordanaires were thrust into the limelight because of a popular newcomer on the rock-and-roll scene. He was a hip-swinging, heart-stopping singer from Memphis, Tennessee, named Elvis Presley, and the musical world has not been the same since. Elvis paved the way for some of the most exciting acts in show business, such as the Beatles and the Rolling Stones. Rock was the craze during the fifties and sixties, and Elvis was considered the king.

The Jordanaires worked with Elvis for nearly fourteen years, and these were exciting times for our group. We were the opening act on all of his concert tours, and we sang with him during his performances. We were in some of his movies and did the sound tracks on most all of them.

Elvis Presley and the Jordanaires in the movie "G.I. Blues."
L to R: Gordon Stoker, Ray Walker, Elvis, Neal Matthews Jr., Hoyt Hawkins.

I like to think of our years with Elvis as the good years of his career. When we quit traveling with him in 1969, his health was still good, and I will always remember Elvis Presley as the most dynamic personality that I have ever witnessed on a stage. We were very fortunate to have worked with him.

When the word spread that the Jordanaires were the background voices on Elvis' early recordings, good things started happening to us. Our association with "the King of Rock and Roll" immediately created a demand for our services as background singers. Before Elvis, we had played some concerts, performed on the Grand Ole Opry, and recorded for Capitol Records. We occasionally did vocal background sessions before our sessions with Elvis, but after a few hits with him, the doors really started opening for us. We became so busy recording background vocals that we were sometimes doing four sessions a day, which requires about sixteen hours during a twenty-four-hour span.

Since most sessions in Music city were "head sessions" — done without written arrangements — during the early years, this began to create a problem for us. Our job as singers was to create a commercial vocal background arrangement, to do it by ear (head arrangement, mostly), to do it efficiently, and to do it in a hurry! The producers were very budget-conscious in those days, and many felt their session was a disaster if they did not record at least four songs in a three-hour session. Many times we would complete six songs in a three-hour session!

The Jordanaires recording with Connie Francis.
L to R: Neal Matthews Jr., Hoyt Hawkins,
Connie, Gordon Stoker, Ray Walker.

Needless to say, the early four-a-day sessions were hectic as we struggled to remember words, intervals, arrangements, and vocal parts. We were forced to rely on hand signals, eye contact, whispering, punching each other, or any other form of communication necessary in order to help each of us to get the job done while keeping our wits together.

Something had to give, and fast! We had endured several months of mass confusion on the one hand, while enjoying escalating success on the other. It was a "good" problem for us because, even though it was frustrating for us at times, we certainly were grateful for the continuing success. Still, something had to be done in order to eliminate the frustration that occurred during the sessions.

Almost every member of our group held a degree in music. But it takes considerable time to write out a vocal arrangement from scratch, and time is most essential when you have so little in a recording session. We were allowed only thirty to forty-five minutes to learn a song, come up with a commercial arrangement, and then convert it into a finished product. Precious time could not be spent writing down four to eight parts for the vocal group. A shortcut was sorely needed. We needed a method of eliminating most of the guesswork and confusion associated with head arrangements or singing by ear. The less we would have to commit to memory, the less confusion we would have to endure. In other words, we needed a compromise between a complete musical arrangement and an arrangement totally committed to memory.

Then the idea came to me. It was just a brainstorm, but it suddenly became a workable solution. Being a former student of the old gospel shape notes, I decided to give each note in the scale a number, the way "Do-Re-Mi" gives each note a sound. Since each of the shape notes had a name plus a corresponding sound for each note in the scale, I simply gave a number to each note in the scale, starting in each instance with 1 as the tonic, or keynote, of the song.

Chords, chord symbols, and related numbers had been used in music since the 1500s, although I was unaware of this at the time. This simple combination of numbers and notes eliminated a lot of problems for us. After developing the basic system further, we were able to read chords and words much quicker, and, by reading numbers instead of panicky hand signals, our head sessions became better organized and much less hectic.

Ferlin Husky, with numerous hit recordings to his credit (such as "Gone" and "Wings Of A Dove"), was one of the first country artists to use the numbers. I used the numbers to write vocal background charts for many of his recordings in the fifties and sixties. Ferlin, who now owns the "Wings Of A Dove" Museum, in Music Village, U.S.A., had this to say about the numbers:

> I guess your numbering system was used on all my recordings — that is, the ones in Nashville. I would see musicians and singers writing down numbers on a piece of paper. I didn't pay that much attention to it — all I know is that it must have worked, because we sure put out some good records without wasting a lot of time!

Ferlin Husky

By eliminating the necessity of using musical notation, the numbering system opened up many doors for anyone who wished to learn new songs in a hurry and wished to learn by ear, either out of necessity or by preference. Thus a new era was born in Nashville that seemed to merge with the development of the "Nashville sound." This was the beginning of the Nashville numbering system, or "Nashville shorthand."

Early Development of the Numbers

The Nashville shorthand is unusual because it works the same in any key. For instance, let us suppose that you wish to play or sing a song in the key of C. Therefore, C is 1, D-2, E-3, F-4, G-5, A-6, B-7, and C-8, or the octave. If you changed keys to F, then F would be 1, G-2, A-3, B♭-4, C-5, D-6, E-7, and F-8, or the octave. We do not use the number 8, however, because it is merely 1 an octave higher, the same as any octave in the scale or any "Do" in the shape-note scale.

For the guitarist, the numbers apply not to the notes of the scale themselves, but to the chords that are named after these notes. Although there are many different kinds of chords, we'll begin by looking at the most basic ones, saving the more complex ones for later.

C			F	G			
1	2	3	4	5	6	7	(8)

The chords on scale steps 1, 4, and 5 are the basic ones for the novice to learn. A singer can sing literally thousands of songs simply by developing an ear for the basic harmony of these three chords. A guitar player can also learn to play thousands of songs by learning these three basic chords, the 1, 4, and 5 chords, and by associating them with the guitar chord symbols in this book. The more you practice, the more you learn. As you can see in the example above, in the key of C the 1, 4, and 5 chords are C, F, and G, respectively. (These are all **major** chords; the other kinds of chords, which we'll look at later, include **minor** and **seventh** chords.)

The Nashville numbering system provided us the shorthand that we needed so that we could depend on our ears rather than on the written arrangement. It took far less time to jot down the chords, and, once you had the chart written, it applied to any key. For example, if you write the numbers down to a song in the key of E, and the artist suddenly decides to raise the song a half step to F, your numbers work for you just the same. You simply sing or play the numbers in F, using F as your 1 chord and moving all others up one half step accordingly. It takes a good ear to do this, but most people have the ability to hear intervals and therefore would be able to adjust to a key change, while the numbers remain the same.

BEAUTIFUL BROWN EYES

Traditional

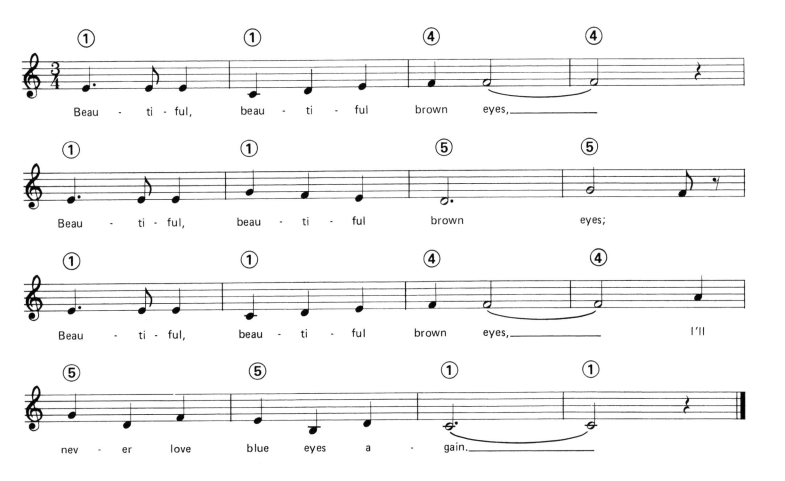

At least seventy-five percent of all the recording sessions in Nashville are "head sessions," therefore using numbers instead of written arrangements. But we will be using the musical staff on occasion in order to demonstrate how the numbers correspond to a given song. It is not necessary to write down the notes of the scale. All I ever do when writing a chart from a demo tape is to write down the numbers and then fill in "oohs," "ahhs," or words whenever necessary. Each number normally represents a bar of music, and I usually space them about two inches apart, with half bars being only an inch apart. This space allows room to write words in the bars when necessary. I usually circle my numbers so the words will not get confused with the numbers. After charting a song in this manner, the only thing left necessary to commit to memory are the intervals we sing, and sometimes we even use numbers to eliminate this problem.

By using this method, very little is left to have to remember, so we can concentrate on intonation and getting the job done. Once you catch on to the system, it takes very little time to chart a song.

BEAUTIFUL BROWN EYES
(number chart)

(1) Beautiful,   (1) beautiful   (4) brown eyes,   (4)

(1) Beautiful,   (1) beautiful   (5) brown   (4) eyes;

(1) Beautiful,   (1) beautiful   (4) brown eyes,   (4)   I'll

(5) never love   (5) blue eyes a-   (1) gain.   (1)

When a producer asked us to sing the entire chorus of a song, I would chart it similar to "Beautiful Brown Eyes," the example above. If you will notice, each word fits into the proper bar, so that it eliminates a lot of guesswork. If your key is C, then you sing two bars of C, two bars of F, etc. If the original key is changed lower or higher, you simply adjust your pitch accordingly, and continue using the same numbers you did in the key of C. Musicians would simply make the new key number 1 and adjust all their chords, never changing numbers. At first, however, the musicians did not use the numbers; that was to come a few years later.

BEAUTIFUL BROWN EYES
(vocal arrangement)

(1) Beautiful,   (1) beautiful   (4) brown eyes,   (4)

(1) Ooh...   (1) ...   (5) ...   (5) ...

(1) Ahh...   (1) ...   (4) ...   (4) ... I'll

(5) never love   (5) blue eyes a-   (1) gain.   (1)

Now let us suppose the producer or artist wanted us to sing "Beautiful Brown Eyes" as it is shown in the previous chart. I would probably say, "voices, sing the first line (1144), ooh the second line (1155), ahh the third line (1144), and sing the last line (5511)." After learning the numbers and vocal intervals, the rest is relatively simple, because it is all on the chart before us.

The beauty of the Nashville sound is that we don't have to read. We don't get locked into an arrangement that we may feel is not as good as one we can improvise. That's what makes the Nashville sound: a free, spontaneous session with the producer, artist, musicians, and background singers all contributing. Someone else would probably have come up with the numbering system here sooner or later, but it sure has made things nice.

Tom Collins, a successful pianist-turned-producer, ranks right at the top of his profession. He has been producing such superstars as Barbara Mandrell and Ronnie Milsap for a number of years and has numerous hits to his credit. Tom's thoughts on the numbers:

> The usage of the numbering system that you (Neal) devised enables a feel to be established without mentally having to think in keys, such as E major, or E minor, or whatever. By using the numbers, you can establish a feel for a song a lot faster, and I think that is one very important ingredient in the success that we've enjoyed in Nashville for years.

One night in 1956, Elvis called us in to hear a song that he wanted to record. He sang it over a couple times, and then I came up with a couple of ideas that he liked, and the arrangement began to jell. The net result was the greatest-selling single record of all time: "Don't Be Cruel" backed with "Hound Dog." Our background chart consisted of a few "bop bops," some unison "oohs," and some four-part "ahhs." The chord chart for a guitar would have been simple on both songs, using only the 1, 4, and 5 chords, with the addition of the 2 minor for "Don't Be Cruel."

Stan Wayman

Elvis and the Jordanaires
(L to R: Gordon Stoker, Hoyt Hawkins, Neal Matthews Jr.).

Mechanics of the Numbering System

A few years after I developed the numbering system, musicians started picking up on it. Although I conceived of the system for our vocal quartet, it spread to all the instruments, the guitar in particular. Some of the new musicians who had just moved into town quickly saw the value of the numbers and adopted the system immediately. Later the older, more established musicians followed suit. David Briggs, keyboard player and producer, and Charlie McCoy, harmonica and guitar player, were probably among the first musicians to use the numbers.

Charlie, who plays almost any instrument, is currently musical director for "Hee Haw" and records for Monument Records. With twelve albums to his credit, his biggest single is "Today I Started Loving You Again." I asked Charlie to give me his viewpoint on the Nashville numbering system:

> When I first came to Nashville in 1959, I came up to audition for some record labels to become a singer, and I was taken to Bradley's recording studio (later CBS) to see a session by Brenda Lee. At that time I was enrolled at the University of Miami as a music education major.

> When I arrived at the session, the Jordanaires were using a notation (numbering) system for chords, and, when I went over, one of the guys explained it to me. To my surprise, it was very similar to what I had been studying in college in music theory. This made me appreciate college more, because I had considered it only a means for formal training. When I went back to school in Miami, my studies were a lot more interesting, because I had seen it being used in commercial music.

> When I came back to Nashville a year or so later, a friend of mine asked me to explain what the Jordanaires were doing, and when I started showing him the numbers, the other musicians saw it and started using it.

> The only thing different about what was being done then and now is that there are now about a hundred different versions of how to write it down. Everybody has their own little version. Some use roman numerals, some have gone to straight-ahead numbers, with different indications of the sevenths, minors, or whatever.

Charlie McCoy

David Briggs, who played piano on several Presley hits and for hundreds of other artists, is now producing and arranging as well as playing on sessions, and is constantly in demand. He owns his own studio, The House Of David, and is currently involved in several projects such as redoing some old tapes of Elvis and Jim Reeves. David had this to say about how he uses the numbering system in his own arrangements:

> I even use the numbers if I don't know the key, to write out little "licks" (fills between phrases on certain instruments). Like one of those things I did for Brenda Lee the other day. I even wrote out the melody in numbers like you (Neal) do all the time. I wrote out the little accents, the eighth notes, or whatever it happened to be, and put the corresponding numbers in the scale so that I could remember it.

> A lot of times I even use it on jingles for guys like Hal Rugg (steel guitar and dobro). For instance, if he's playing stuff like that slide dobro, which is so hard to play, you just write something out in numbers with the accents and he reads enough music that he'll play the part right. It saves having to teach somebody the part, and it saves a heck of a lot of time, besides reminding you of the melody, because you know that a lot of times we don't even need to know the key we're in!

> I just did a network jingle for Maxwell House Coffee, and I wrote the whole thing out in numbers, melody and all. I use it beyond just the chords — I use it with notes and everything. Some guys have a little trouble reading, so the numbers help, but the guys who read well use my numbers with no problems, and the little accents and fills that I write out with numbers they pick up in a hurry. Numbers — I can't do without them!

Many veteran observers are still amazed at the speed and skill with which the musicians can hear a song once and get it down on paper. Nashville pickers even talk in shorthand. You may hear a leader yell "eleven forty-four twice, twenty-two fifty-five, and fifteen eleven." It sounds like a quarterback barking out signals at the line of scrimmage, but in reality it is probably the first verse of a song.

Once the numbers spread throughout the Music Row community, everyone seemed to adopt his own style of using them. The instrumentalists do not enclose their numbers in circles, as I do, and they don't need as much space, since they do not have to write the words. Thus, 1144 would constitute four bars of music and takes very little space. A musician's chart on "Beautiful Brown Eyes" would be: 1144 1155 1144 5511. Or, some would write it like this:

(Verse)	(Chorus)	(Verse)
1144	1144	1144
1155	1155	1155
1144	1144	1144
5511	5511	5511

There is no set way to write it, but I prefer the method above. As you can see, a musician who wished to conserve paper could conceivably write the chord numbers to a whole album on one sheet of paper by using this system. There is no juggling to find the right manuscript, no turning pages when the arrangement is long. You simply write your numbers down on a sheet of paper, and you are set for the day!

As I stated earlier, the Nashville numbering system evolved from the "Do-Re-Mi's." As a matter of fact, because of its popularity, the major scale (Do Re Mi Fa Sol La Ti Do) has become a standard method of understanding and expressing music. But in order to learn more about the major scale, you must first become acquainted with another scale: the chromatic scale.

The chromatic scale consists of twelve notes from "Do" to "Do," instead of the seven that make up the major scale. Each of these twelve notes is a half step from the next. A half step is the distance from one fret to the next on the guitar.

In examining the following diagram, you will undertand the relationship between the seven notes of the major scale and the twelve notes of the chromatic scale.

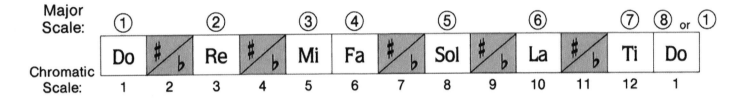

There is a whole step (two half steps) between each note of the major scale and the next, except between 3 and 4 and 7 and 8. Any note played in between the other natural (numbered) notes of the major scale would be called either a sharp (♯) or a flat (♭). A half step higher than a natural note makes it a sharp. For example, a half step higher than a C would be C sharp, or C♯. In the key of C, there is only one half step between E and F (3 and 4) and B and C (7 and 8), so you use F (4) and C (8) rather than E sharp and B sharp.

A half step lower than a natural note makes it a flat.

The overall sound of the major scale is the same in any key because of the distribution of whole and half steps. They will be in the same order, no matter what key you are in.

In the key of C, all the notes are natural, with no flats or sharps. In the other keys, however, the distances between the notes in whole and half steps require some sharp or flat notes. For example, in the key of F, if you played the notes F G A B C D E F, you would find that between A and B (3 and 4) there is a whole step, which is wrong. Now, flat the B note and the scale becomes F G A B♭ C D E F, which is correct. With the exception of C, all keys have sharps or flats; these are indicated at the beginning of a song by the key signature:

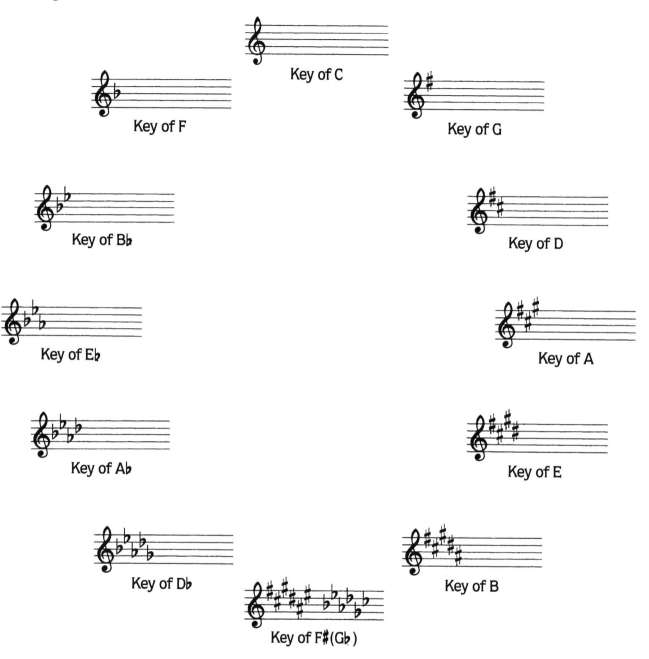

A sharp or flat note can be cancelled at any time by a natural sign (♮). It is written to the left of the desired note, and it tells you that the natural note is needed instead of the previous sharp or flat. This sign also affects all notes in the same position that follow in that measure. The natural sign, and the key signature itself, are seldom used in the Nashville numbering system, since notes normally are not written down.

Just as there are twelve notes in the chromatic scale, which together include all of the notes of the major scales in all keys, so there are only twelve major chords that you need to know in order to play the basic 1, 4, and 5 chords in any key.

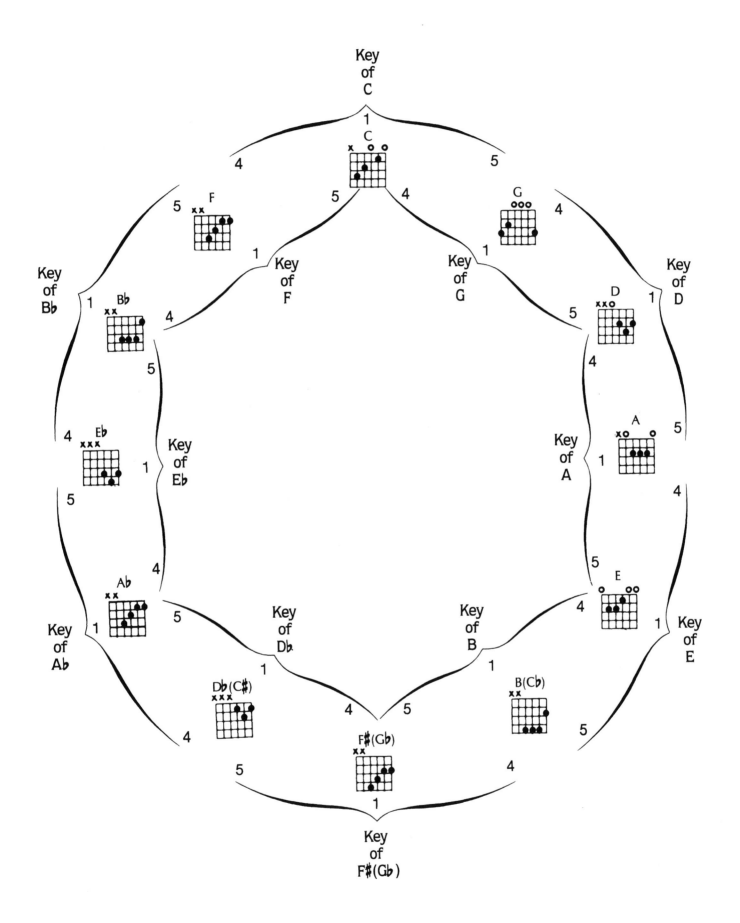

One of Elvis' first million-sellers was "Heartbreak Hotel," written by Mae Boren Axton, Tommy Durden, and Presley himself (BMI) and published by Tree International. This song is a good example of using the 1, 4, and 5 chords to build a complete song. In the numbering system, a musician would chart "Heartbreak Hotel" like this:*

HEARTBREAK HOTEL

$\frac{4}{4}$ medium time   Key of E

‖: 1	1	1	1^7		
4	4	5	1		
1	1	1	1^7		
4	4	5	1	:‖	
(Guitar break) 1	1	1	1^7		
(Piano break) 4	4	5	1		
1	1	1	1		
4	4	5	1	⌢*	*Means to "hold" the ending longer than written.

*The number chart, which is based on the recording, differs from the notated version on the next page; this is not unusual. For an explanation, see page 52.

HEARTBREAK HOTEL

Words and Music by MAE BOREN AXTON,
TOMMY DURDEN and ELVIS PRESLEY

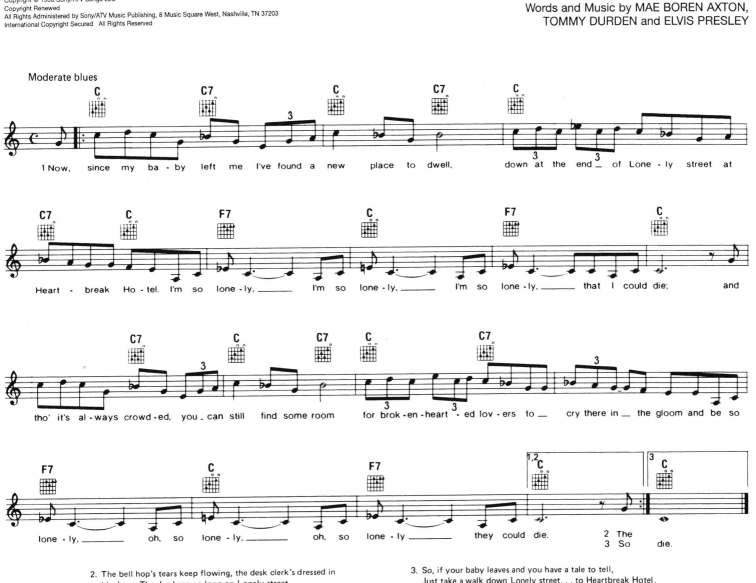

Moderate blues

1 Now, since my ba-by left me I've found a new place to dwell, down at the end_ of Lone-ly street at

Heart-break Ho-tel. I'm so lone-ly, _____ I'm so lone-ly, _____ I'm so lone-ly, _____ that I could die; and

tho' it's al-ways crowd-ed, you _ can still find some room for brok-en-heart-ed lov-ers to _ cry there in _ the gloom and be so

lone-ly, _____ oh, so lone-ly, _____ oh, so lone-ly _____ they could die.   2 The
3 So die.

2. The bell hop's tears keep flowing, the desk clerk's dressed in
black . . . They've been so long on Lonely street,
They never will go back. . . and they're so lonely. . . Oh, they're
so lonely . . . they're so lonely . . . they pray to die.

3. So, if your baby leaves and you have a tale to tell,
Just take a walk down Lonely street. . . to Heartbreak Hotel,
Where you'll be so lonely. . . and I'll be so lonely . . . We'll be so
lonely . . . That we could die.

If a leader were calling out chords for the other musicians, he would probably say, "No intro, 1111⁷, 4451, 1111⁷, 4451 — now, repeat that much; then a guitar break on 1111⁷, and a piano break on 5511. Then 1111⁷, 4451 with an ending on the third beat of an extra bar of 1. It's in $\frac{4}{4}$ time in the key of E. Here's the tempo; let's go!" Sound crazy? Perhaps, but those instructions would have been enough for the musicians to chart the entire arrangement of "Heartbreak Hotel."

Building Chords by the Numbers

The most basic chords consist of three notes; these notes generally are taken from the scale of whatever key the song is in. For example, let's return to our old friend the C major scale, and compare it to the basic three-note C major chord.

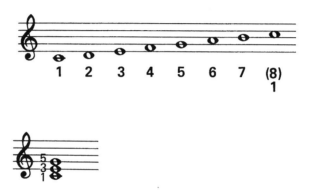

The three notes of the C major chord are numbers 1, 3, and 5 of the C major scale. Coincidentally, when we speak of the distances between the notes of a chord — called "intervals" — we use these same numbers. The bottom note of the chord, for which the chord is named (C in this case) is called the **root**. The next note is called the **third** of the chord, because it lies at the interval of a third above the root. In this case, it is a **major** third, which equals two whole steps, and which gives the chord the name **major**. The next note of the chord is the **fifth,** so called because it lies at the interval of a fifth (three whole steps and a half step) above the root.

Next, let's look at the three-note versions of the 1, 4, and 5 chords that are the basic chords used in country music.

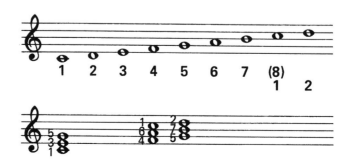

22

Although the numbers of the notes differ from chord to chord (1 3 5, 4 6 1, 5 7 2), the intervals between the notes are the same: in the 4 chord, from 4 to 6 is a major third (two whole steps), and from 4 to 1 is a fifth (three whole steps and a half step); the same is true in the 5 chord, with the interval from 5 to 7 being a major third, and the interval from 5 to 2 being a fifth.

These three major chords — 1, 4, and 5 — form the basis of a lot of music, from country to classical to rock. But they are not the only chords used. Let's look at the chords that are built on the remaining notes of the scale.

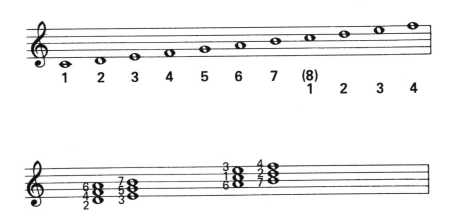

The 2, 3, and 6 chords are called **minor** chords, since, instead of major third (two whole steps) between the root and third of the chord, they each have a minor third (a whole step and a half step). the 7 chord is kind of an orphan; it is called a **diminished** chord (because the fifth is not a true or "perfect" fifth of three whole steps and a half step, but a "diminished" fifth of two whole steps and two half steps), and it is rarely used.

One amazing thing about the numbering system is that each musician has his own way of using it. My method is somewhat different than those of some musicians, because mine is used for voices. The musicians, once they learn the basic steps, create their own methods. That is the beauty of the system — you too can create your own method.

For example, I would write the following four bars like this: 1 6ᵐ 2ᵐ 5, with lots of space in between. A musician would write it 1 6- 2- 5. The minor sign can be written 1min, 1ᵐ, or 1-; so take your choice. We will use the dash in our charts so as not to be confusing. On pages 34 and 35 you will find charts showing the different chord types and corresponding numbers most often used in country, rock, and pop music.

My intention is to keep the numbering system as simple as possible, so that accomplished musicians can develop their own methods as far as they wish, and yet those who either do not read or who read very little can pick the system up without any trouble and have fun in the process.

In a simple song involving three-note chords, the root of the chord could be on the bottom, in the middle, or on the top of the chord, depending on the melody of the song itself. For example, from the point of view of the backup singers, we may jot down $\frac{5}{3}$ in the first bar, which simply means we would sing the notes 1-3-5 of the particular key we are in, with 5 being the top note. Should we decide to change intervals, we would simply adjust our notes, such as $\frac{1}{5}$ or $\frac{3}{1}$

In a more complicated song, other notes can be substituted or added to form augmented chords, suspensions, and other variations. Some of these require more than three notes, however, and we will cover those later.

Elvis Presley and the Jordanaires had a common love for spirituals and gospel songs. In fact, this is what originally brought us together as a team. I especially remember one night on a recording session with Elvis at the RCA studio. The session officially started at 6 p.m., but Elvis sat down at the piano and we sang spirituals for hours. The producers were practically out of their minds. It was costing them thousands of dollars, but no one dared approach Elvis about the matter.

Suddenly, about 3 a.m., Elvis jumped up to the mike and said, "Okay, all you guys get out your pads and scribble down some numbers for this song, 'cause I'm ready to roll!" Within one hour we had written a number chart and had finished cutting "Crying In The Chapel," one of Elvis' many RCA hits. Needless to say, RCA more than recovered its investment.

Elvis also loved to kid us about the numbers. One day at a session he said "I can never get these guys to work. All they want to do is play games with numbers. I can't figure out whether they're working puzzles or playing tic-tac-toe!"

L.A. Todd

Elvis and the Jordanaires in the recording studio.
Standing, L to R: Gordon Stoker, Hoyt Hawkins, Neal Matthews Jr., Hugh Jarrett.
Seated at the piano: Elvis.

CRYING IN THE CHAPEL

Words and Music by
ARTIE GLENN

CRYING IN THE CHAPEL

Slow $\frac{4}{4}$

Voice intro: You saw me crying in the

A	4^6	4^6	1	1
	2	4-/5	1/4	1✓ *

B	4^6	4^6	1	1
	2	4-/5	1/4	1/1⁷

C	4/4-	1/6-	2	⟨5⟩**
	4^6	4^6	1	1
	2	4-/5	1/4	1/1⁷

4/4-	1/6-	2	⟨5⟩
4^6	4^6	1	1
2	4-/5	rit.◇	1

* 1 ✓ Break on the 1 chord (stop strumming) and hold until the 2 chord. This is the symbol I use.

** ⟨5⟩ Some musicians use this to signify a break. It is called a diamond, and it means that either one, some, or all break on the first beat. In the song above, everyone broke on the first beat. If there is no chord enclosed, the diamond signifies a whole-bar rest.

Jerry Reed and his lovely wife, Priscilla, have been our friends for years. Priscilla sang with us some during the early years, and Jerry was a "session guitar picker" before Chet Atkins decided to "make him a star," and star he is!

Jerry has not only had numerous hits on RCA, but now has several hit movies to his credit with friend and co-star Burt Reynolds. Jerry says this of the numbers:

Why didn't I think of that myself. It makes everything so much simpler, a number for every note in the scale. By the way, Neal, I forgot you thought that up. Thank you, hoss!

Transposing and Modulating

Transposing and modulating both have to do with changing keys. Transposing is moving a song from the key it was written in to some other key. The most common reason for transposing is so that the song "fits" the singer's voice better. Modulating is changing keys within a song. This is done to add variety or excitement to the performance.

By thinking of chords as a progression of numbers rather than of letters, you can transpose any chord progression from any key to any other. Simply replace the letter name of the chord or note in the original key with the letter name of the chord or note that has the same number and falls in the same vertical column on the Major Key and Number Chart on page 29. 1, 2, 3, 4, 5, 6, 7, 8 (1) represent the tones of the major scale, while the flats and sharps, such as 3♭, 7♭, 5♯, represent the altered tones.

For example, suppose you were charting sixteen bars of a song in the key of C:

C	F	G7	C		1	4	5^7	1
C	C7	F	F		1	1^7	4	4
F	D-	C	A-	**or**	4	2-	1	6-
D-	G7	C	C		2-	5^7	1	1

These chords could fit the first verse of hundreds of songs in country music. Let's suppose that the song is much too low in the key of C, and you wish to move it up a fourth to the key of F. Simply replace the letter name of the C chord by finding F in the first column. Then the F chord becomes the 1 chord and you use the Key Chart once again to find the rest of the chords. To find the next chord, find the 4th step of the scale at the top of the chart, move down to the F row, and there you will find B♭. The next chord is a 5^7, so find the 5th scale step at the top, work down to the F row again, and you will find a C^7 chord. The fourth bar repeats the 1-F chord:

F	B♭	C7	F		1	4	5^7	1
F	F7	B♭	B♭		1	1^7	4	4
B♭	G-	F	D-	**or**	4	2-	1	6-
G-	C7	F	F		2-	5^7	1	1

Major Key and Number Chart

1	1# / 2b	2	2# / 3b	3	4	4# / 5b	5	5# / 6b	6	6# / 7b	7	(8)1
C	C# / Db	D	D# / Eb	E	F	F# / Gb	G	G# / Ab	A	A# / Bb	B	C
Db	D / Ebb	E	E / Fb	F	Gb	G / Abb	Ab	A / Bbb	Bb	B / Cb	C	Db
D	D# / Eb	E	E# / F	F#	G	G# / Ab	A	A# / Bb	B	B# / C	C#	D
Eb	E / Fb	F	F# / Gb	G	Ab	A / Bbb	Bb	B / Cb	C	C# / Db	D	Eb
E	E# / F	F	F× / G	G#	A	A# / Bb	B	B# / C	C#	C× / D	D#	E
F	F# / Gb	G	G# / Ab	A	Bb	B / Cb	C	C# / Db	D	D# / Eb	E	F
F#	F× / G	G	G× / A	A#	B	B# / C	C#	C× / D	D#	D× / E	E#	F#
Gb	G / Abb	A	A / Bbb	Bb	Cb	C / Dbb	Db	D / Ebb	Eb	E / Fb	F	Gb
G	G# / Ab	A	A# / Bb	B	C	C# / Db	D	D# / Eb	E	E# / F	F#	G
Ab	A / Bbb	B	B / Cb	C	Db	D / Ebb	Eb	E / Fb	F	F# / Gb	G	Ab
A	A# / Bb	B	B# / C	C#	D	D# / Eb	E	E# / F	F#	F× / G	G#	A
Bb	B / Cb	C	C# / Db	D	Eb	E / Fb	F	F# / Gb	G	G# / Ab	A	Bb
B	B# / C	C	C× / D	D#	E	E# / F	F#	F× / G	G#	G× / A	A#	B
C	C# / Db	D	D# / Eb	E	F	F# / Gb	G	G# / Ab	A	A# / Bb	B	C
1	1# / 2b	2	2# / 3b	3	4	4# / 5b	5	5# / 6b	6	6# / 7b	7	(8)1

Modulating by the numbers is easy, and the guitarist should have no problems. Modulating can be up or down, by half steps, whole steps, fourths, fifths, or any other interval, but the most common modulations in country music are up by either a half step or a whole step. This is true in rock and pop music as well. Going up one half step adds excitement and a sense of climax, especially on the last chorus or fading choruses of the modern country or pop song.

There are several ways to modulate from one key to another by the numbers. Using the last four bars of the previous sixteen-bar verse (2-5^7 1 1), let's modulate one half step up. We will do this by replacing the last 1 chord with a 5♯ transitional chord. (2- 5^7 1 5♯ 1♯). This would lead us into a new key one half step higher. The 1♯ chord in the old key now becomes the 1 chord in the new key, and the numbers remain the same except each chord from that point on is played one half step higher.

Let's go up a whole step using the same example. It would be 2-5^7 1 6^7 2. The 2 chord of the old key now becomes the 1 chord of the new key. Then you use the same patterns and numbers to finish the song one step higher.

Modulating Up a Half Step

F	B♭	C7	F	1	4	5^7	1
F	F7	B♭	B♭	1	1^7	4	4
B♭	G-	F	D-	4	2-	1	6-
G-	C7	F	(C♯)	2-	5^7	1	(5♯)
F♯	B	C♯7	F♯	1	4	5^7	1
F	F♯7	B	B	1	1^7	4	4
B	G♯-	F♯	D♯-	4	2-	1	6-
G♯-	C♯7	F♯	F♯	2-	5^7	1	1

Modulating Up a Whole Step

F	B♭	C7	F	1	4	5^7	1
F	F7	B♭	B♭	1	1^7	4	4
B♭	G-	F	D-	4	2-	1	6-
G-	C7	F	(D7)	2-	5^7	1	(6^7)
G	C	D7	G	1	4	5^7	1
G	G7	C	C	1	1^7	4	4
C	A-	G	E-	4	2-	1	6-
A-	D7	G	G	2-	5^7	1	1

Another method of modulating is simply to move into the new key at a certain point during the song without using a transitional chord. Should you wish to move up a step, for instance, without using the transitional 6^7 chord, you would simply move to the 2 chord, which then becomes a new 1 chord. Then all your numbers are the same as they were except that you are playing chords one step higher from the point of modulation.

Common Modulations

Up a Half Step

original key:	1	5	1	5♯ (1♯)	
new key:				1 4	1 1

With a 5♯ transitional chord, 1♯ in the original key becomes 1 in the new key.

Up a Whole Step

original key:	1	5	1	6 (2)	
new key:				1 4	1 1

With a 6 transitional chord, 2 in the original key becomes 1 in the new key.

Without a Transitional Chord

original key:	1	5	1	1 (2)	
new key:				1 4	1 1

You can modulate up smoothly, either a half step or a whole step, without a transitional chord.

Up a Fourth (Two and One Half Steps)

original key:	1	5	1	1^7 (4)	
new key:				1 4	1 1

With a 1^7 transitional chord, 4 in the original key becomes 1 in the new key.

Transposing and modulating become second nature with the numbers. Once the numbers are charted, they never change, no matter what key you are playing in, unless you use one of the transitional chords to help move you to another key.

The Nashville musicians are the best and the quickest in the world at using numbers for this purpose.

The major scale sounds the same in any key, and this helps in relating numbers to chords and keys. In order to find a comfortable key for the artist, musicians must be able to transpose, maybe even several times, during a session. They can do this because their ears are tuned to numbers that correspond to certain chords. In a new key, they start all over with the same numbers that correspond to new chords.

Without a good ear this is difficult. However, most guitarists acquire a good ear and use numbers instinctively even though some may not be aware of it. As we progress, we will be showing some hit songs with sheet music and numbers. Play along using the Key Chart (page 29) until you know the numbers. Try transposing to another key. You're already on your way!

Buddy Killen, along with Jack Stapp (now deceased), built Tree Publishing Company into the largest country music publishing company in the world. Buddy started out in Nashville playing bass fiddle on the Grand Ole Opry in the 1950s, so he helped greatly in building the Nashville sound. He is now not only President of Tree International, but is also a very successful producer, recording such outstanding artists as T.G. Sheppard and Ronnie McDowell. Buddy says:

> The numbering system has meant a great deal to me as a producer because the musicians know the chord structure initially, and if we have to change keys they don't have to transpose. It is a great time-saving device and easy for everyone to play.

Larry Butler writes for Tree Publishing Company and is not only an accomplished writer, but also a talented pianist and one of the top producers in the music field. Among his writing credits are "Another Somebody Done Somebody Wrong Song" with Chips Moman. He produced Kenny Rogers' "The Gambler," Billie Jo Spears' "The Blanket on the Ground," Mac Davis' "It's Hard to be Humble," Don McLean's "Crying," John Denver, B.J. Thomas, Kenny Rogers and Dottie West duets, Sammy Davis Jr., Paul Anka, Steve Lawrence and Eydie Gorme, Charlie Rich, and Julie Andrews! Larry said this about the Nashville numbering system:

> The numbering system is sort of in compliance with the old system of Nashville recording. It allows all of the musicians to be able to have the freedom to know what the chord is with the additional freedom to play what they feel should be played along with the song. Instead of reading notes or music that is written out in every detail, they are reading the basic chord change and they can use their own particular skills and contribute to the record itself.

> The greatest part about it is if you have a key change, or if the artist at the last minute is not comfortable with a certain key, it only takes a matter of a few seconds to change keys, and before, you had to rewrite the entire music for each player.

> I use the numbering system a lot in writing songs. If I happen to write a song in the key of A, and it is more comfortable in B♭ when I get to the studio, the numbers still apply.

During the Tree Publishing Company Christmas brunch in December 1982, Buddy Killen presented Larry Butler with the Decade Award. This award signifies one of the top ten songs in money earnings for Tree during the past decade. The song commemorated was "Another Somebody Done Somebody Wrong Song."

Hope Powell

Larry Butler (L) receiving the Tree Decade Award from Buddy Killen.

33

Building New Chords

By altering major chords, we are able to add many new sounds to our basic formula in the numbering system. For example, to change a major chord to minor, you simply flat the third. Instead of a major 1 3 5, you would then have a minor 1 3♭ 5. To make the same chord a minor seventh, you simply add a 7♭ to it. Thus, to take the example of a Cm7 chord, you would have C E♭ G B♭.

The following charts show some variations of the basic chords you have learned thus far. In addition to listing the name of a chord and showing the formula in numbers needed to build it, the charts show the chord symbols most often used and the styles in which you might expect to find that kind of chord. By following the charts, you can improvise and design your own chords by the numbers.

Type of Chord and Formation by Numbers	Chord Symbols (Based on C)	Musical Styles in which Used
MAJOR CHORDS		
Major 1 3 5	C, 1	Country, Pop, Folk, Gospel, Rock, Bluegrass
Major Sixth 1 3 5 6	C6, 1^6	Country, Folk Gospel
Major Seventh 1 3 5 7	Cmaj7, CΔ7 1maj7, 1Δ7	Country, Classical, Jazz, Pop
Major Ninth 1 3 5 7 9	Cmaj9, CΔ9 1maj9, 1Δ9	Jazz, Classical, some Country
Major Add Nine 1 3 5 9	Cadd9, C9 1^9	Country, Jazz
Suspended Fourth 1 4 5	Csus4 1sus4	Gospel, Country, Rock

Type of Chord and Formation by Numbers	Chord Symbols (Based on C)	Musical Styles in which Used
MINOR CHORDS		
Minor 1 3♭ 5	Cmin, Cm, C- 1m, 1-	Country, Folk, Rock, Bluegrass, Gospel, Pop
Minor Sixth 1 3♭ 5 6	Cmin6, Cm6, C-6 1m6, 1-6	Country, Pop, Rock
Minor Seventh 1 3♭ 5 7♭	Cmin7, Cm7, C-7 1m7, 1-7	Country, Classical, Latin, Rock, Pop
Minor Ninth 1 3♭ 5 7♭ 9	Cmin9, Cm9, C-9 1m9, 1-9	Country, Jazz, Pop, Classical
Minor, Major Seventh 1 3♭ 5 7	Cm(M7), Cm(+7) 1m(M7), 1m(+7)	Pop, Jazz
DOMINANT CHORDS		
Seventh 1 3 5 7♭	C7, 1^7	Country, Folk, Pop, Rock, Jazz
Ninth 1 3 5 7♭ 9	C9, C7add9 1^9, 1^{7}add9	Country, Rock, Gospel, Pop
Seven Flat Nine 1 3 5 7♭ 9♭	C7♭9, C7-9 1$^{7♭9}$, 1$^{7-9}$	Jazz, Pop, Classical
AUGMENTED, DIMINISHED CHORDS		
Augmented 1 3 5♯	Caug, C+ 1aug, 1+	Country, Pop, Jazz, Gospel
Diminished Seventh 1 3♭ 5♭ 7♭♭	Cdim7, C°7 1dim7, 1°7	Jazz, Classical (no Country)

Refer to these formulas as you study the different types of chords shown on the following pages. We will show the basic chords on the staff, as well as the guitar chord forms, for several chords on all twelve steps of the chromatic scale.

Major Chords

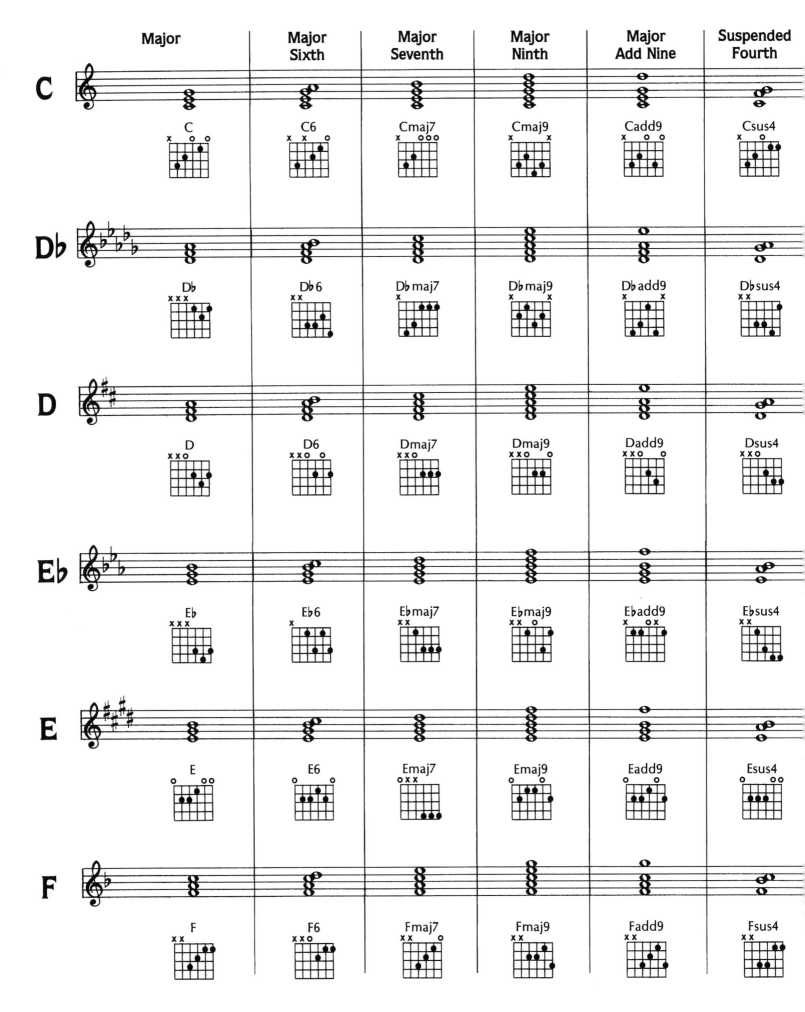

Major Chords
(continued)

Minor Chords

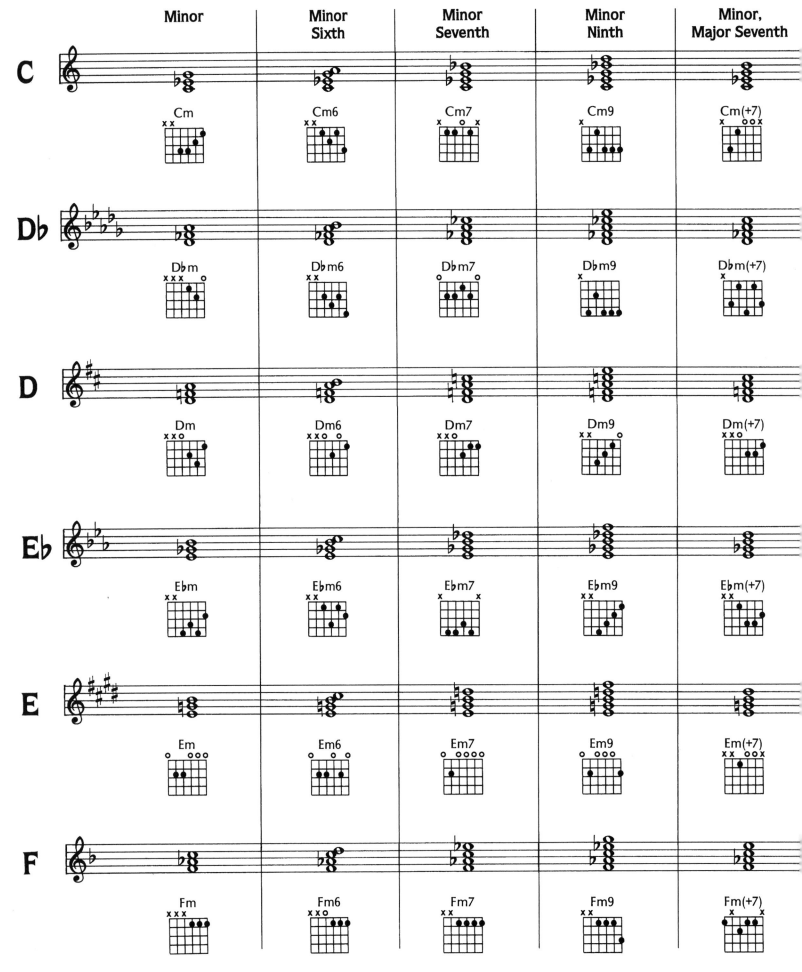

Dominant Chords

Augmented, Diminished Chords

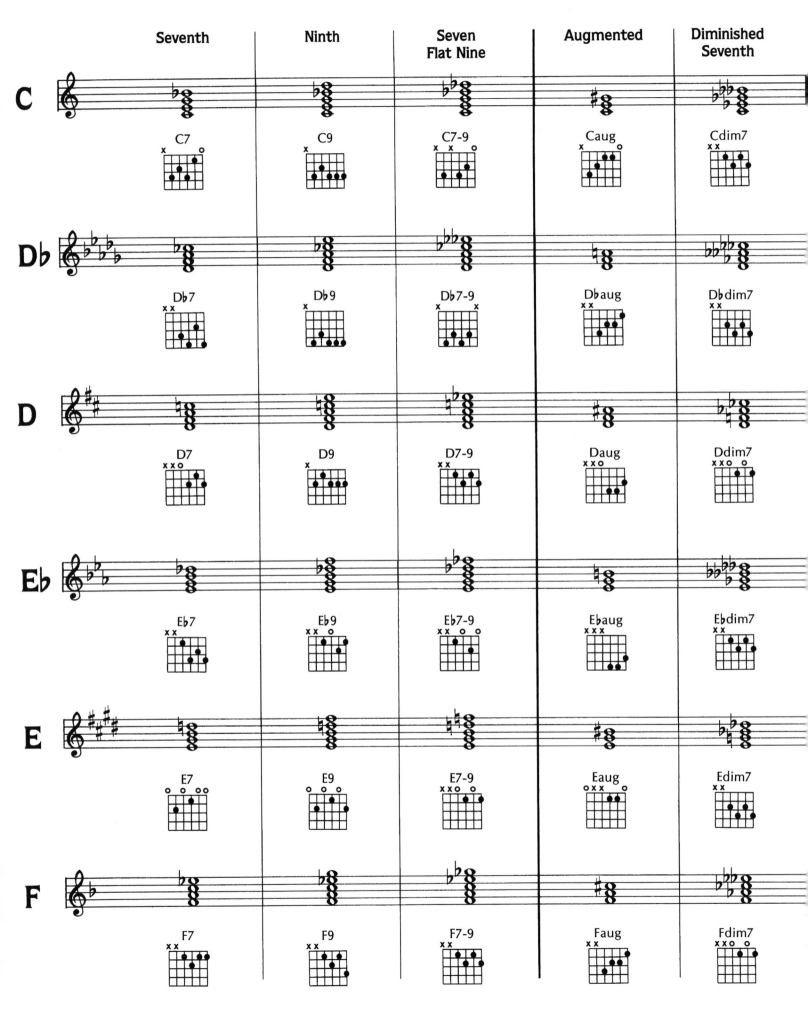

Dominant Chords
(continued)

Augmented, Diminished Chords
(continued)

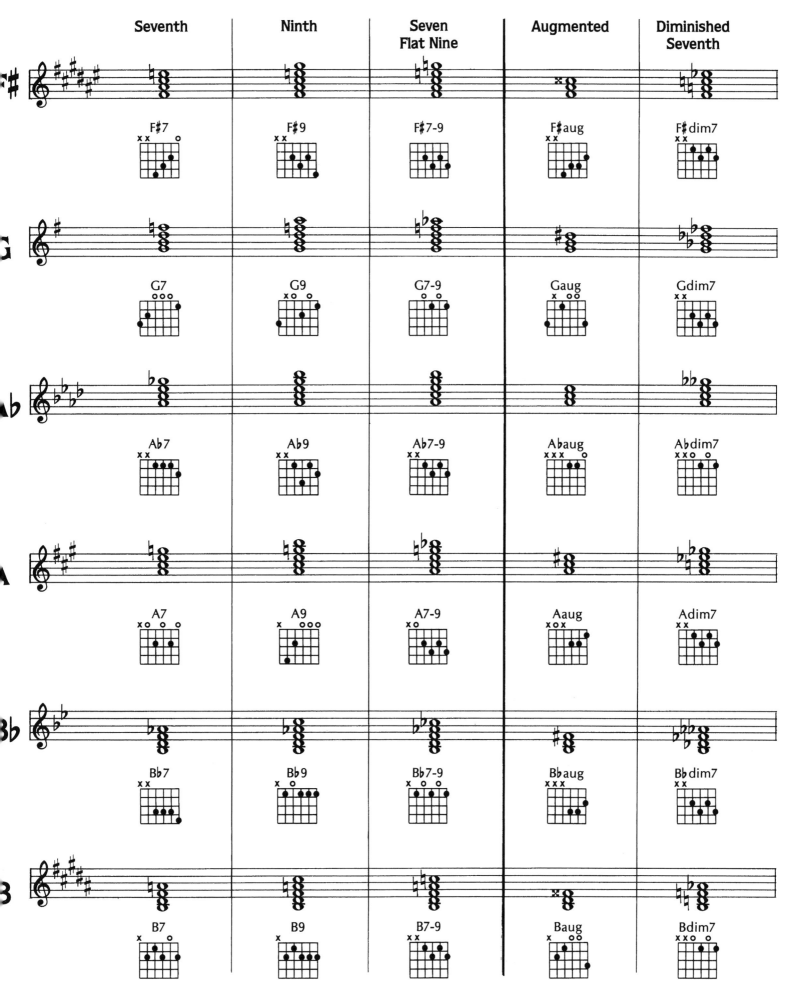

Owen Bradley was one of the pioneers of the Nashville sound. He and brother Harold bravely left downtown Nashville to venture out to 21st Avenue, and then later to 16th Avenue to build the first recording studio on what is now called "Music Row." Bradley studios were later purchased by Columbia with the understanding that not one ashtray be moved, because they did not want to change the good sound of the studios.

A few years later, Owen converted an old red barn in Mt. Juliet, Tennessee, into a recording studio. There, he produced hit records for such notables as Patsy Cline, Loretta Lynn, Conway Twitty, and Bill Anderson, just to mention a few.

Owen had this to say about the numbering system:

> When I was just a kid I played in a band and we used a numbering system of sorts, but it was not very well organized.
>
> When you (Neal) came along with your system, you actually refined it and got it down to a point where it really is marvelous. I guess it is so simple in a way that I wish someone had discovered and explained it to me sooner!
>
> It is one of the best things that has happened to Nashville to solidify our system of playing, It made such an impact by making it so easy to switch from one key to another, and you don't have to rely on memory so much.

Loretta Lynn presenting Owen Bradley
with a Gold Record for "Coal Miner's Daughter," March 1982.

Harold Bradley, Owen's brother, is not only a businessman, but also one of the original early-fifties creators of the Nashville sound. Harold is an accomplished guitarist as well as a successful independent producer. Here are some of his comments to me:

I had studied numbers in college, but they were roman numerals, and I had forgotten it. I can remember that you were the first one to use the numbers, and a few years later the musicians started picking up on it. For a while, I would notice you and the Jordanaires huddled in the corner with a pad and pen, but didn't know you were writing numbers for quite a while.

At first I was totally against the numbers because I did not think I could get the feel of a song using numbers.

However, as the music became more complicated, and as I moved into a leadership role, I found that the numbering system was great. It gives you a point of reference. In the past, we always had to play everything over from the top if there was any confusion on a chord. Now, with the numbers, we simply call out the number in question and straighten it out, therefore eliminating confusion.

It is a tremendous time saver. Anything that can save you fifteen minutes could mean a hit song. The greatest example of the numbers was on a Fred Waring session at the Sound Emporium Studio five or six years ago. I put my arrangement on the music stand, and it started on the floor to my left and ended on the floor to my right. I quickly called the producer over and asked if he would wait a minute. I folded up my six-page guitar arrangement, walked over to the piano and asked Bill Purcell to play the song one time for me. As he played, I wrote down the numbers on the blank back side of my folded arrangement. It took less than one-half page to chart the entire song. I can even remember the song. It was the Johnny Cash song "Daddy Sang Bass" (made popular by Cash, but written by Carl Perkins).

My only regret is that, had we thought about it earlier, maybe we could have standardized it in some way. I myself write across in sixteen-bar phrases. Some guys write down the page four bars at a time. We may use different methods, but we usually come up with the same numbers.

Vicki Carr came over after we finished her album and said, "Can I have your numbers sheet? You guys are not in the music business, you're in the numbers racket! I want to take this back to the arranger who will write the strings in Hollywood, and say, 'There it is, write it!' " She did take it back to Hollywood, handed it to the arranger and he said, "What in the world is this?"

Language of the Recording Studio

As I stated earlier, my methods of writing numbers will vary some from those of instrumental musicians, and instrumentalists themselves have methods that vary from one to another. Once it started spreading, everyone seemed to chart his own course, although there are similarities, so we'll start from there.

Below are charts comparing how I write for background voices and how a guitarist would write the same song.

GREEN GREEN GRASS OF HOME

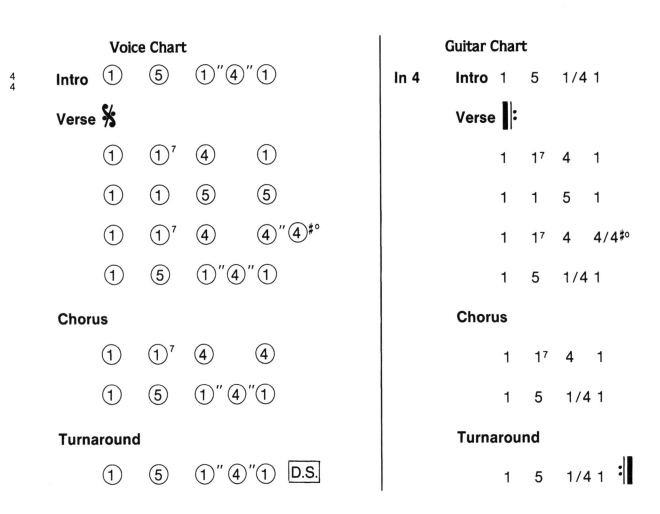

GREEN GREEN GRASS OF HOME

Words and Music by
CURLY PUTMAN

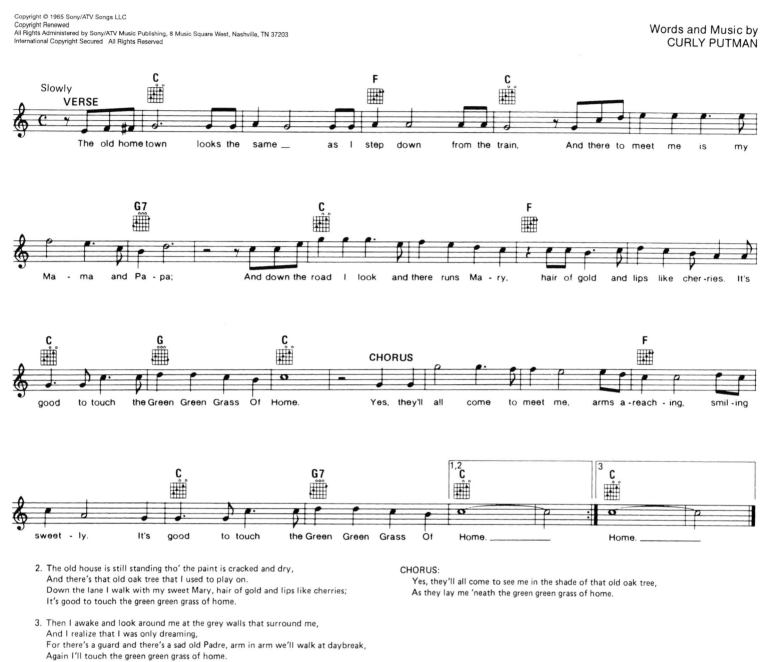

2. The old house is still standing tho' the paint is cracked and dry,
   And there's that old oak tree that I used to play on.
   Down the lane I walk with my sweet Mary, hair of gold and lips like cherries;
   It's good to touch the green green grass of home.

3. Then I awake and look around me at the grey walls that surround me,
   And I realize that I was only dreaming,
   For there's a guard and there's a sad old Padre, arm in arm we'll walk at daybreak,
   Again I'll touch the green green grass of home.

CHORUS:
   Yes, they'll all come to see me in the shade of that old oak tree,
   As they lay me 'neath the green green grass of home.

As you probably have noticed, the number charts contain some abbreviations. On the following pages we will cover most of the signs musicians commonly use in the numbering system.

TIME: Country music mainly uses $\frac{4}{4}$ time, $\frac{2}{4}$ time, $\frac{3}{4}$ time, and $\frac{6}{8}$ time. $\frac{6}{8}$ time means six beats to a measure and is actually a fast waltz. $\frac{3}{4}$ time is three beats to a measure (waltz) and is usually done slowly, as in the "Tennessee Waltz." $\frac{4}{4}$ time, four beats to a measure, is used the most. Its tempo is usually moderate to fast, with the emphasis on two and four. Slow it down real slow and you get into $\frac{2}{4}$ time — two beats to a measure. Another extremely popular rhythm is commonly known as "straight eighths," which is $\frac{4}{8}$ time. If a $\frac{4}{4}$ feel doesn't work, the rhythm guitars will play eighth notes, strumming up and down with equal emphasis on each note.

$\frac{4}{4}$ (In 4) $\frac{2}{4}$ (In 2) $\frac{3}{4}$ (In 3) $\frac{6}{8}$ (In 6)

ROUTINES: We are always asking each other, "What's the routine of that song?" This simply means how many verses, choruses, turn-arounds, or what is the breakdown of the song? Songs usually come in eight- or sixteen-bar phrases, with one or two verses, then perhaps a chorus, and then another verse or a release, which is the last half of a verse. Then it may have a turnaround, and repeat the bridge and the release, or another verse, then a tag, and out!

Do routines sound complicated? They really aren't. On our note pad we would write down the routine to the song like this before taking down the numbers:

> V(16)
> V
> ___
> C (Includes Release)
> ___
> Turn. (Turnaround)
> ___
> C
> ___
> Tag (last 4)

Two Ways of Writing a Routine

In 3	No Intro					$\frac{3}{4}$ time	No Intro				
Vs	‖:	1	6-	2-	5		1	6-	2-	5
		1	1	4	4		1	1	4	4	**A**
		4	4-	1	6-		4	4-	1	6-
		2-	5	1	1 :‖		2-	5	1	1
Cho 𝄋										
		4	4	1	1		1	6-	2-	5
		2⁷	2⁷	5	5		1	1	4	4	**B**
Release							4	4-	1	6-
		1	1	4	2		2-	5	1	1
		5	5	1	1 ⊕					
					To Tag	𝄋				
Turnaround										
		5	5	1	1 D.S.		4	4	1	1	**Cho**
Tag ⊕		5	5	1	1 ⌢		2⁷	2⁷	5	5
							1	1	4	2	**Rel**
							5	5	1	1

1. Instrumental
   5   5   1   1   D.S.

2. Tag
   5   5   1   1   ⌢

SPLIT BARS: Bars in which more than one chord is played are called "split" bars; they can be split on any beat that calls for a new chord. The most common would be a split $\frac{4}{4}$ bar with a chord change in the middle of the bar. An example would be 1 5 1/4 1. The third bar is split, with two beats on the 1 chord and two beats on the 4 chord. If you wanted to play three beats of the 1 chord and only one beat of the 4 chord, you would chart it this way: 1 5 (⁑ . . ⁴) 1. The three dots signify three beats on the 1 chord above, and the one dot signifies one beat only for the 4 chord. Look for these split bars in the songs that appear in the following chapter.

For Guitar:	1	5	1/4	1		1	5	(⁑..⁴)	1
For Voices:	①	⑤	①"④"①			①	⑤	①'''④'①	

SIGNS: There are enough signs used by most of us so that you can use them in developing a composite system of your own:

Repeat signs — ‖: :‖ These signs are placed at the front and the end of any phrase you wish repeated. They are used by most musicians, although I also like to use the D.S. sign, which returns you back to this sign: 𝄋 , wherever it is placed. We also write little notes, such as REPEAT TO TOP, REPEAT BRIDGE, or REPEAT CHORUS.

Letters — Some routines are charted in letters; these are normally eight-bar, twelve-bar (usually blues), or sixteen-bar phrases. A typical example would be letter A (8 or 16 bars) or first verse; letter B (8 or 16 bars) or second verse; letter C (16-bar chorus).

Some typical studio talk:

- "Take it from the top." (Go back to the beginning.)

- "Let's go up a half at the bridge." (Modulate up one half step at the end of the first bridge.)

- "It's not there yet." (That certain feel that the artist or producer needs is not there. Perhaps the key is wrong, the tempo, or the arrangement.)

- "It's a take!" (What everyone is looking for! — an acceptable tape.)

- "Tag the last four." (Usually means to repeat the last line of the song.)

- "Diamonds on letter B." (Play the first chord of each bar in letter B and let them sustain.)

- "Okay, let's hook it!" (Let's wrap it up this time.)

- "You're dragging the bridge." (Someone, usually the drummer, is slowing the tempo at the bridge.)

- "One more before we lose it!" (Sessions are based on a certain feel. Each song has to build to that certain climax, and everyone can usually tell when it's there. It's like building momentum at a football or basketball game. You don't want to lose it!)

In all of the number charts in the following chapter, we will strive to be consistent in the signs. After all, we want the numbers to be fun to play.

Jerry Bradley, former Division Vice President of Nashville Operations for RCA Records, has produced such notable country music stars as Charley Pride, Dottie West, Dave and Sugar, Nat Stuckey, Johnny Russell, and Jimmy Dean. Jerry's thoughts on the numbering system:

> From the business standpoint of making the records, and having recorded in other parts of the United States and the world, I can see the value of the numbers. It enables you to do things quicker, and that affects the bottom line. If you can record in Nashville, do it quicker, and do it well, then it becomes a definite plus from a business point of view.

> I was still emptying ashtrays at dad's (Bradley's) studios (now CBS), even before Kris Kristofferson, when the numbers started. He went on to become a movie star, but the business has also been good to me!

> One of the reasons I like to record in Nashville is, for example, if you want to change keys, everybody is ready to go. You go somewhere else and you lose that.

> I've been in London on occasion with Briggs (David, pianist and producer), and I watched from the control room as he showed them the numbering system. I've seen other artists who were intrigued, and, once they saw how it was done and how simple it is, they would say, "Now, why didn't I think of that?"

> I believe it was John Denver who was really impressed with the numbering system. While recording in Nashville, he came up to see me and it seems we had quite a lengthy conversation discussing numbers and about how much he loved recording in Nashville!

Jerry has had an outstanding career. Aside from the artists mentioned already, he signed such stars as Alabama, Ronnie Milsap, and Sylvia to the RCA label. He was also responsible for the now-famous "Outlaws" album (Willie Nelson, Waylon Jennings, Jessi Colter, and Tompall Glaser). It started the outlaw trend and was the first country album to be certified platinum, which means one million copies were sold.

Don Putnam

Jerry Bradley (L) and Charley Pride.

B.J. Thomas has been a great artist for a number of years. Among the better-known hits to his credit are "Raindrops Keep Falling on My Head" and "Another Somebody Done Somebody Wrong Song."

B.J. on the Nashville numbering system:

> The Nashville music charts (numbers) are the only way to go. That way the musicians immediately know their parts, things go faster, and with the numbers they are not limited to just the songs with written charts. They can record any song that we can think of right on the spot.

> When they (the musicians and singers) have a song to listen to, they have a chart immediately! I thought at one time they couldn't read music, but in essence it frees them up to be really creative because they are not limited to just the musical score. The Nashville numbering system has always made it possible to cut more records quicker while allowing everyone to be more creative on the session.

Pete Drake, owner of "Pete's Place" recording studio, has played a vital role in the development of the Nashville sound. Pete is a steel guitar player who has played on untold numbers of hits over the years. He is also a successful producer, with many hit records to his credit from such stars as B.J. Thomas, Melba Montgomery, Ernest Tubb, and most of the other acts on the Grand Ole Opry roster. Pete's remarks about the numbers:

> In 1969 I went over to England to play steel on the album "All Things Must Pass" with George Harrison and the Beatles. They are used to playing a song over and over until you learn the chords, so they said they would play it a few times until I learned it. They ran it down once and I said, "I've got it!" They said, "No, you couldn't have it," but I yelled, "Yeah, I got it! Play and I'll show you!" They were amazed and said, "How in the world did you do that?" Then I showed them the Nashville shorthand and I told them that you (Neal) came up with it.

> The Beatles asked me to show it to them, so I sat down and showed them the 1144s and the 5511s. Their songs had a lot of unusual chords that you could not possibly remember unless you wrote them down, and it really shocked them the way it was done. They would listen to the playbacks and write out the numbers. They caught on quickly and were so amazed at how simple it was that one of them made the remark, "Now why didn't we think of this?"

> A year later, I produced Ringo Starr on an album in Nashville, and he still was astonished when he saw all the musicians pull out pads and pencils to write down numbers at the beginning of the session!

B.J. Thomas

Pete Drake

Hit Songs by the Numbers

This chapter contains several hit songs that have been country standards over the years. Some are old and some are new, but you will probably recognize most of them.

We will attempt to analyze several of the chart routines so that you can easily understand how to chart verses, choruses, know when to repeat bridges and other phrases, and, in general, know exactly how to write the numbers.

We will also include some sheet music so that you will be able to compare the numbers with the chords on the sheet music. Sometimes they will vary because the number charts are taken from the actual recording of the song and not from the sheet music. Sheet music — even that sold in single copies or in books in music stores — is often simplified compared to the recording itself. Such simplified versions are often called "lead sheets" ("lead" is pronounced "leed").

In a recording, songs may include intros, turnarounds and even additional chords that may not appear on a lead sheet, so listen for these chords when practicing taking down charts from records, and look for the differences between the following lead sheets and number charts.

KING OF THE ROAD

$\frac{4}{4}$ feel

Med. tempo

Intro (bass fiddle and snaps)

				Routine:
1	4	5	5	A
				B
1	4	5⁷	1	Cho
1	4	⟨5⟩	◇	A
1	4	5⁷	1	A*
1	4	⟨5⟩	◇	

*Fade on A with bass fiddle and snaps.

Analysis of the chart:

- $\frac{4}{4}$ time with $\frac{4}{4}$ feel. (Equal emphasis on all beats.)

- Notes on intro self-explanatory.

- Diamonds on 5 chord in seventh bar of each eight-bar phrase. This means to stop on first beat, and wait through next complete bar.

- Split bar, end of letter B. Two beats on 1 chord and two beats on 5♯ leads into chorus which will be one half step higher from then on.

- D.S. or Return to sign (letter A). The routine says to play letter A again, then all instruments drop out except bass fiddle; then fade.

All of this was charted on less than half a page!

KING OF THE ROAD

Words and Music by
ROGER MILLER

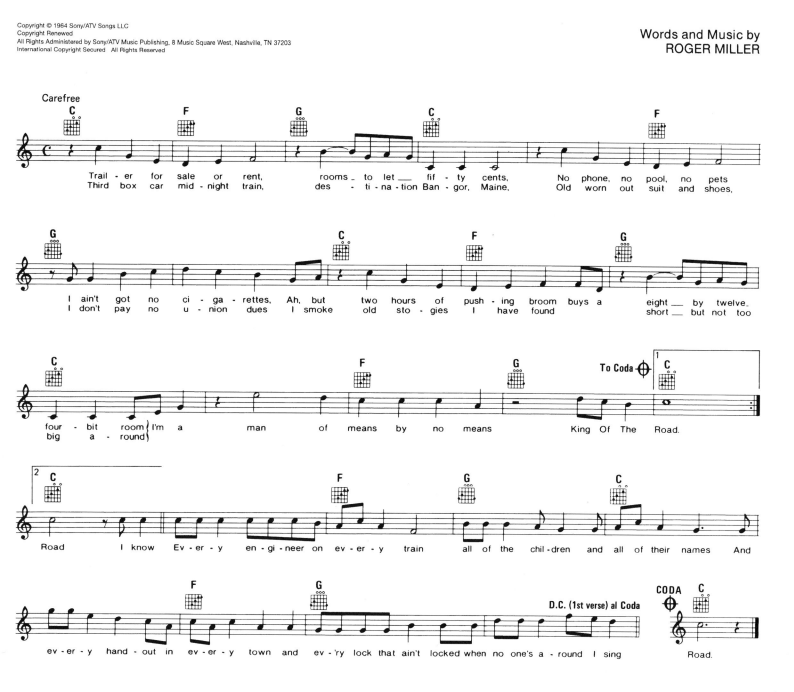

(Hey Won't You Play)
ANOTHER SOMEBODY DONE SOMEBODY WRONG SONG

$\frac{4}{4}$ No Intro

Diamonds on Elec. Piano

ad lib.

<1>   <4>   <5>   ◇

a tempo   guitars

<4>   ◇   1   1

Cho	1	$1^\triangle$	1^7	1^7
	4	4	1	1
	2-	5	1	1
Vs 𝄋	1	1	3	3
	6	6	2	2
	5	5	1	6^7
	2	2	5	5
Cho	1	$1^\triangle$	1^7	1^7
	4	4	1	1
	2-	5		
Instr	1. 1	$1^\triangle$	1^7	1^7
	4	4	1	1 D.S.
Cho (Fades)	2. :∥ 1	$1^\triangle$	1^7	1^7
	4	4	1	1
	2-	5	:∥	Fade 2nd x

Analysis:

- Electric piano only until sixth bar. Tempo is established by voice in fourth bar.

- Rhythm guitars in at sixth bar.

- Play to first ending.

- Instrumental for eight bars.

- Return to sign, play 2nd ending and fade on 2nd ending.

These are the instructions a producer would give prior to recording this song.

(Hey, Won't You Play)
ANOTHER SOMEBODY DONE SOMEBODY WRONG SONG

Words and Music by LARRY BUTLER
and CHIPS MOMAN

HE STOPPED LOVING HER TODAY

$\frac{4}{4}$ Mod. Tempo

1-bar vocal pickup

Analysis:

- No intro; vocal pickups into letter A.

- Play through A, B, and first ending.

- Return to sign for repeat and take 2nd ending.

HE STOPPED LOVING HER TODAY

Words and Music by BOBBY BRADDOCK
and CURLY PUTMAN

Moderately

VERSE

He said, "I'll love you 'til I die", She told him, "You'll for-get in time." As the years went slow-ly
He kept some let-ters by his bed, dat-ed nine-teen-six-ty-two; He had un-der-lined in

by, she still preyed up-on his mind; He kept her pic-ture on his wall
red ev-ery sin-gle "I love you"; I went to see him just to-day,

and went half-cra-zy now and then; But he still love her through it all, hop-ing she'd come back a-gain.
but I did-n't see no tears; All dressed up to go a-way;

[2,3]

First time I'd seen him smile in years. _

CHORUS

He Stopped Lov-ing Her_ To-day; They placed a wreath_ up-on his door; _____

And soon they'll car-ry him a-way; _____ He Stopped Lov-ing Her To-day. _____

To Coda

D.S. (3rd ending) al Coda   CODA

Verse 3
(Recite)

She came to see him one last time
We all wondered if she would
And it kept running through my mind
This time he's over her for good. (REPEAT CHORUS)

MAMMAS DON'T LET YOUR
BABIES GROW UP TO BE COWBOYS

$\frac{3}{4}$ Med. Tempo

Intro (Rhythm vamp)

	1	1	1	1					
Cho	1	1	1	1	4	4	4	4	
	5^7	5^7	5^7	5^7	5^7	5^7	5^7	1	1
	1	1	1	1	4	4	4	4	
	5^7	5^7	5^7	5^7	5^7	5^7	1	1	1 1

Vs ‖:	1	1	1	1	4	4	4	4	
	5^7	5^7	5^7	5^7	1	1	1	1	
	1	1	1	1	4	4	4	4	
	5^7	5^7	5^7	5^7	5^7	5^7	1	1	1 1

Cho	1	1	1	1	4	4	4	4	
	5^7	5^7	5^7	5^7	5^7	5^7	5^7	1	1
	1	1	1	1	4	4	4	4	
	5^7	5^7	5^7	5^7	5^7	5^7	1	1	1 1 :‖

Fade Cho.

Analysis:

- Four-bar rhythm vamp into first chorus.
- Play through Cho, Vs, Cho to repeat sign.
- Go back to first repeat sign and repeat Vs and Cho.
- Fade on Cho.

MAMMAS DON'T LET YOUR BABIES GROW UP TO BE COWBOYS

Words and Music by ED BRUCE
and PATSY BRUCE

Additional Verse

A cowboy loves smokey ole pool rooms and clear mountain mornings,
Little warm puppies and children and girls of the night.
Them that don't know him won't like him and them that do sometimes won't know how to take him.
He's not wrong he's just different and his pride won't let him do things to make you think he's right.
(Repeat Chorus)

BLUE

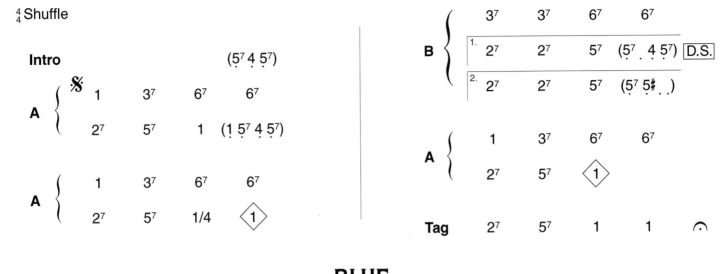

BLUE

Words and Music by
BILL MACK

MAKE THE WORLD GO AWAY

Slow 4/4 Vocal pickup

Cho	2-	5	1	1	
	2-	5	(1..2-)	◇1	
Vs	5	5	1	1	
	4	5	1	◇1	
Cho	2-	5	1	1	
	2-	5	(1..2-)	◇1	
Vs	5	5	1	1	
	4	5	1	◇1	
Cho	2-	5	1	1	
	2-	5	(1..2-)	1	
Tag	2-	5	1	1	𝄐

MAKE THE WORLD GO AWAY

Words and Music by
HANK COCHRAN

Do you re-mem-ber when you loved me / hurt you, before the world took me a-stray? / I'll make it up day by day. If you do, then for-/Just say you love me like you

give me, / used to, And Make The World Go A-way. Make The World Go A-way. and get it off my

shoul-ders, say the things you used to say, and Make The World Go A-way. I'm sor-ry if I

61

I FALL TO PIECES

$\frac{4}{4}$ Shuffle

Intro ‖: 4 5 1 1

1 4 5 $(\dot{5}..\dot{5}\flat)$

4 5 1 1

A 1 4 5 $(\dot{5}..\dot{5}\flat)$

4 5 1 1

1^7 1^7 4 4

5^7 5^7 1 1

B 4 5^7 1 1

4 5^7 1 1 :‖

Tag 4 5 1 1

I FALL TO PIECES

Words and Music by HANK COCHRAN
and HARLAN HOWARD

Broadly

Fall ___ To Piec - es ___ each time I see you a - gain. ___
Fall ___ To Piec - es ___ each time some - one speaks your name. ___

Fall ___ To Piec - es; ___ How can I be just your friend? ___ You
Fall ___ To Piec - es; ___ Time on - ly adds to the flame. ___ You

want me to act like we've nev - er kissed; ___ you want me to for - get, pre-tend we've nev - er met; ___ And I've
tell me to find some - one else to love, ___ some - one who'll love me, too, the way you used to do; ___ But each

tried ___ and I've tried, but I have - n't yet; ___ You walk by and I Fall To Piec - es. ___
time ___ I go out with _ some - one new; ___ You walk by and I Fall To Piec - es. ___

1. 2.

62

BOOT SCOOTIN' BOOGIE

Additional Verses

2. I've got a good job, I work hard for my money.
   When it's quittin' time, I hit the door runnin'.
   I fire up my pickup truck and let the horses run.
   I go flyin' down that highway to that hideaway
   Stuck out in the woods to do the boot scootin' boogie.

3. *Instrumental*

4. The bartender asks me, says, "Son, what will it be?"
   I want a shot at that redhead yonder lookin' at me.
   The dance floor's hoppin' and it's hotter than the Fourth of July.
   I see outlaws, in-laws, crooks and straights
   All makin' it shake doin' the boot scootin' boogie.

Final Note

The history of the Nashville numbering system turned out to be as interesting as the system itself. Renewing old memories with lots of friends made the work seem like play and the whole endeavor quite enjoyable.

My quartet partners and friends for many years, Gordon Stoker (tenor and manager), Hoyt Hawkins (baritone, now deceased), and Ray Walker (bass since 1958), have shared many fond memories and experiences working with most of the top artists in country, rock, and gospel. They have contributed greatly in the building and improving of the numbering system over the years.

Gordon: I studied numbers at OBU (Oklahoma Baptist University), and I have a book at home. While growing up I remember singing the melody and chords on the piano by reading the roman numerals above each chord change from the sheet music my sister would buy. I think they are still using roman numerals in some sheet music.

A lot of people laughed at us about the numbers. They thought we were playing around, I guess, but when they found out how swift it was, they all started jumping on the bandwagon. We used it about five years before anyone started picking it up.

Ray: Using numbers allows us freedom to feel our music and to improvise our harmonies, since we are not tied to the written notes. Parts and voicing are easily altered by simply pointing up and down, and knowing which part to sing according to the key is second nature to us, because the numbers are the same in all keys. Therefore we have empathy with the spirit of the music, otherwise known as soul. Also, we get to sing what we know best and the way we know best when not confined to a written arrangement.

The numbering system has meant a lot to us over the years. It has not only opened lots of doors for us, but has provided us an instrument to use even in some faraway places that has really caused some eyes to pop! We sometimes take it for granted in Nashville because most everyone in the recording business has used it for years, and this gives me a great deal of satisfaction.

It's a shortcut, it's a time-saver, and it's relatively simple; and, in recalling another statement by Gordon Stoker, "It keeps a line of communication open between us as a vocal group and the musicians that no written chart can."

Music should be fun, and whether it is used as a hobby or to make a living, it should be interesting to you. If this system has helped you improve your method of playing the guitar or any other instrument, improved your "ear," or just made it easier to enjoy music in general, then our efforts have not been in vain.